To CAROLYN

Best Wishes

My Native Land
By Owen Duffy

Jock Whitelaw

ISBN 978-0-9568545-0-6

i

MY NATIVE LAND

Acknowledgments

John Whitelaw, Friend, Editor and Publisher
for making it all happen

Frank McCormick Artist, Ian Craig Graphic Designer

The Staff at Scottish Printing Services Scotland
Ian Chisnall Managing Director
Avril Reid Office Adminitration
Carol Hunter Assistant
Back Room Boys John Hay, Michael Wright

Shirley Nelson and Laura Butcher for their assistance
in typing and e-mailing material

For Book

John Whitelaw for funding First Edition

And lastly to the people of Kelty from by-gone days for providing
the inspiration for this book.

Owen Duffy March 2011
First Published 2011
Artwork Frank McCormick
Printed by Printing Services (Scotland) Ltd, Dunfermline
Typesetting, Layout and Design by Ian Craig, Printing Services (Scotland) Ltd

Contents

MY NATIVE LAND

Foreword

Audrey S Kinnersley
Head teacher
Clentry Nursery
Kelty, Fife
Scotland

In recent press, it was reported that Clentry Nursery is recognized as one of the best in the country and received a glowing HMI report and several awards for its groundbreaking work.

With a poem in your head, anything can happen. A poem can transport you in an instant from your everyday surroundings to fantasy lands. Poems can also bring you closer to home, by capturing a feeling from the past, whether it be humorous or sad.

Through the talents of author Owen Duffy and artist Frank McCormick (who sadly passed away after being diagnosed with cancer.) My Native Land brings to the reader an insight into life in years gone by. They describe events, real and mythical, using a mixture of real life, love and humour.

From ~The Making of Scotland, The Loch Ness Monster, Kelty, My Native Land, Bruce and The Spider, The Greatest Scot and finally The Bagpipes, Owen Duffy proudly describes to the reader, memories of his homeland.

Appealing to families currently living in Scotland, My Native Land will also attract a wide readership from Scottish people living abroad, particularly in Canada, where the author has lived for fifty five years.

Wherever the words take you and whatever you glimpse there, the poems of Owen Duffy will evoke memories, themes and messages from the past of our parents and forefathers of bygone years.

Audrey S Kinnersley
March 2011

COMIC VERSES

The Making of Scotland

In the beginning when the world was being created

God was in his chambers
Working on some plans
When in came angel Gabriel
With spare time on his hands

What are you doing Lord
Gabe said it with affection
I'm creating a new country said God
Without an imperfection

You are full of anticipation
But you'll see when my plan is unfurled
I'm creating Scotland a brand new nation
The best country in the world

It will be a beautiful land
One you will adore
Its beaches will have lots of sand
And many miles of shore

Majestic mountains that reach the sky
Forests with greenery
A haven where all birds can fly
Amid this scenery

It will have spacious glens
Filled with purple heather
A place where men can be men
And clans can get together

It will have coal in the ground
And oil beneath the sea
A haggis that is plump and round
A nectar they call tea

Its golf courses will be lush and green
And rivers filled with fish
A promised land fit for a Queen
As good as you can wish

There's nothing bad I must confess
But just you wait and see
I'll put a monster in Loch Ness
And bagpipes that seem off key

Hold on God I know your kind
And your giving Scotland lots
But your giving the best of all mankind
Don't you think your too generous to these Scots

No, I will do them one more favour
Though Scotland is a gem
Wait till you see the interesting neighbour
That I'm giving them

A LEADING LIGHT

Robert Burns was a humble man
A wise and noble sage
He wrote poems with great Elan
Of Scottish heritage

His tartan heart was staunch and true
The thistle was his flower
For Scotland's sake he'd drink a few
On any day or hour

He would always help, that was his trait
No matter what the call
He did it well with no debate
This Scotsman he stood tall

Though many years have come and gone
His star it still shines bright
Give him his due his words live on
He's still a leading light

Longing For the Real World

I don't care for the world as it is
With it's buses it's planes or it's trains
the highways and cars I never would miss
I'd get out if I had the brains

But I'm caught up in this modern race
Where we vie to be king of the hill
And slowly but surely I'm losing the pace
I think that I've had my fill

I long for Scotland midst forest and streams
Where flowers bloom every spring
Where rivers run deep fulfilling my dreams
And birds forever will sing

Where tall tree's stand majestic in light
Tranquillity covers the land
Where friendships grow and all is right
Just with the shake of a hand

Grass will be lush, a beautiful green
And robin's splendid in red
Magnificent views the best ever seen

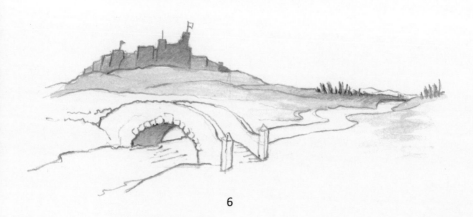

The Greatest Scot

There was a man named Robert Burns
His nickname was Rabbie
And though he was from Lowly Stock
His mind was not too shabby

He wrote poems and songs
Songs of Jubilation
He wrote the song Auld Lang Syne
That is sung in every nation

William Wallace used a claymore
When in a highland fight
His life was filled with blood and gore
It was not a pretty sight

Wallace came in second
He had led a Scottish horde
His glory also beckoned
But the pen was mightier that the sword

For in a recent survey test
To find the most famous of the lot
Robert Burns was rated best
And named the greatest Scot

No One Has Seen a Live Haggis

This is a story that few people know
It started in the highlands, many years ago
Up in the hills, that's where they thrive
So the story said
But no one's seen a haggis live
They've only seen them dead

Night time is like a dark abyss
When light is almost gone
And that is what the gloaming is
Between the dusk and dawn

And so one special night each year
It happens in the fall
The reason isn't really clear
Why the haggis come to call

But down they come, out from the hills
To march across the glen
Their shrieking and their wailing, chills
The Blood in Scottish men

But the highlanders are steady
It is their battle zone
They're in the trenches ready
And lie there still and prone

The haggis they are running free
Across the pitch black glen
And being dark of course can't see
The trenches or the men

They come up to the battle seat
And step across the crest
A highlander he grabs their feet
And ends their midnight quest

His left hand holds them kicking
His right hand holds a knife
Then he starts it flicking
And takes the haggis's life

For hours the battle it goes on
They are dying by the score
And by the time daylight dawns
The haggis are no more

Now you've heard the story
Remember what was said
No one's seen a live one
Cause the haggis are all dead

The Pipe Band

The skirl of the pipes
Kettle drums that roll
The measured steps, kilts that sway
TI's music to my soul

Bonnie Dundee, Scotland the Brave
The music is loud and clear
It washes over me like a wave
And soothes my inner ear

When I hear the bagpipe strains
No feelings are denied
Blood it rushes in my veins
And fills my heart with pride

The Loch Ness Monster

Down in the deep dark murky depths
As black as any tomb
Far below a creature stirs
Amid the dank and gloom

For in the waters of Loch Ness
Where daylight's never been
In an underwater cavern
Lives a monster seldom seen

She's over forty feet in length
This Serpent of the Sea
A body with tremendous strength
And soul that must be free

Her life is one of solitude
Down on the ocean floor
A place where mortals can't intrude
And where no eagles soar

Though few have ever seen her face
Her fame has spread worldwide
She comes and goes without a trace
Yet fills our hearts with pride

For in the waters of Loch Ness
Amid the foliage green
In an underwater cavern
Lives a monster, Scotland's Queen

14

My Native Land

when I'm walking on the strand
Of a far and distant land
It's not hard to understand
Why I love Scotland
And no matter where I go
I want the world to Know
That I think that it is grand
My native land

There's a land across the sea
That is very dear to me
And my thoughts are running free
To bonnie Scotland
And no matter where I roam
Over land or sea or foam
It will always be my home
Bonnie Scotland

It's a land where people care
Where its heroes do or dare
And the heather grows so rare
In bonnie Scotland
And the folk who come to mind
Are so wonderful and kind
They're the best you'll ever find
In bonnie Scotland

There are times I like to dream
Of a fast flowing stream
And the waters as they gleam
In bonnie Scotland
But when all is said and done
I am still a native son and there's really only one
Bonnie Scotland

Bruce and the Spider

King Robert the Bruce sat in a cave
His army was depleted
Six times he had fought a royal war
Six times he was defeated

Sitting there morose and sad
His kingly dreams diminished
The world he knew had turned out bad
He felt his life was finished

It was then he saw a spider appear
Up on the cavern hall
Trying to spin a web so sheer
Across from wall to wall

Six times it tried, six times it failed
There was no use denying
No matter what result entailed
The spider kept on trying

It tried again a seventh time
Across the hall it swung
It made it to the grit and grime
And to the wall it clung

The king saw this , he was amazed
He thought his quest had ended
And though he was confused and dazed
His thoughts he quickly mended

He knew he must try once again
To gain the Scottish crown
This time he won at Bannockburn
Gained fame and world renown

The moral of this story
Is when you feel like crying
Remember Bruce and the spider
And never give up trying

KINGDOM of SCOTLAND

Scotland

Scotland's a small country
Just a thumbnail on a map
But it gives us the Loch Ness monster
And even Andy Capp

Simpson gave us Chloroform
To take away the pain
And MacIntosh the raincoat
To save us in the rain

Television was invented
By Baird as you can tell
Robert Burns wrote poetry
And Scottish songs as well

James Watt gave us the steam engine
So we could travel far
Macadam gave us roadways
Made with stones and tar

Alexander Graham Bell
He did a lot of talking
He invented the telephone
To save lot of walking

James VI authorized translation of the Bible
Although he was very rich
Patrick Ferguson invented the breech loading rifle
That works without a hitch

Scotland is a country
As small as you will find
But it gave us these inventors
To benefit all mankind

When You Feel Important

Into this crazy world of ours
We mortals come and go
Just like the hazy April showers
And cold winter's snow

So when you feel important
And better than your friend
Remember this, before you rant
And people you offend

Just fill a pail with water
Put your hand in, to the wrist
The hole that's left, when you take it out
Is how much you'll be missed

When I Go To Heaven

When I go to heaven
My first surprise will be
Seeing peoples faces there
I didn't expect to see

The second wonder I am sure
Will be faces that are missing
The ones I thought were good and pure
Who spent life reminiscing

The third most wonderous of all
Will bring me to my knee
Is waking up in Heaven's hall
And finding little old me.

God Does Not Like People

God is all supreme they say
He knows all things we do
He created everyone from clay
With different points of view

He made us in his image
if scriptures we believe
But when I look around me
That's not what I perceive

If God did like people
Which we tell ourselves so smuggly
Then why did he make us feeble
And many of us so ugly

A Point of View

There was a flood in the valley
A man was in his home
His name was MacInally
And he lived there all alone

The water was deep it continued to rise
It reached the window sill
A boat came by just the right size
With one space ready to fill

A voice yelled, jump in and we'll save you
The man he replied with a grin
I've trusted the lord all my life
This isn't the time to give in

The water grew deeper and deeper
It reached the second floor
The man thought God is my keeper
He'll save me and settle the score

Time went by he continued to wait
There was water all over the place
The man stood up so tall and Straight
No fear upon his face

A boat came by, a voice yelled, we'll save you
The man he replied with a grin
I've trusted the Lord all my life
This isn't the time to give in

By this time the water had now reached the roof
To the chimney he clung for dear life
He believed in God without any proof
Cause the saviour had helped him through strife

He still had that wonderful feeling
When you believe in the things that you must
And although his senses were reeling
He still felt in God he could trust

A boat came by and a voice yelled, we'll save you
The man he replied with a grin
I've trusted the Lord all my life
This isn't the time to give in

Water now covered the valley
The house it vanished from view
Death came and claimed MacInally
He went to a heavenly pew

He said to St. Peter, excuse me my man
I want an audience with The Lord
St. Peter replied you certainly can
Because that's all you can afford

His meeting with God was a wonderful sight
He was angry and said with a frown
All of my life I have followed your light
And yet you let me drown

My son said God, your death is a shame
But you don't have the overall view
It's not my fault, and I'm not to blame
I sent three boats to save you

Adam & Eve

Adam he lived near the jungle
T'was the time when life just began
He thought the good Lord had bungled
In creating, just one lonely man

He noticed the lion and the lioness
How they would frolic and run
How animals when at their recess
Were having so much fun

The gorilla would swing from the branches
His mate would climb up a tree
They all had their romances
The only one left out was he

He noticed all this, felt he couldn't win
For he was the one all alone
He wondered if he had committed a sin
And to God for this must atone

And then one night he decided
To ask God to help with his fate
God's feelings were hurt, he felt chided
But agreed to give him a mate

Now, God gave Adam a warning
That out of the woods he must bide
And when Adam awoke the next morning
He found lovely Eve by his side

He wasted no time, taking Eve by the hand
They went in the woods just to play
But he wanted more, you must understand
Not caring what God had to say

A short time later Adam ran out
And shouted oh Lord for my sake
Please tell my why and all it's about
What in the world's a headache

Why There Are Ten Commandments

Moses was on the mountain
He was very very sad
His people who had once been good
Had started to turn bad

They were lying, They were cheating
And killing people dead
Had bad manners while eating
No matter what he said

So Moses thought that he would ask
The Lord God for His aid
It isn't quite an easy task
To make bad habits fade

A Voice came down and then God said
I know just what you need
A commandment is the very thing
to turn your men from greed

Moses said, oh Holy one
How much will it be
The Lord replied to you my son
It's absolutely free

Moses said I thank you Lord
And thank you for my men
And since the price I can afford
I think that I'll take ten

The Wrong End

A lady once sat down to eat
In a restaurant one day
A waiter he came to her seat
To serve her if he may

She asked the waiter then to bring
The best food he did vend
And he replied that tongue's the thing
That he would recommend

Tongue, she cried out in disgust
I'm not from the south
I would not even eat a crust
That's from an animal's mouth

The waiter he was humble
His face it turned beet red
But managed still to mumble
What will you have instead

The woman was in happy voice
She'd made the waiter beg
Then she said I've made my choice
I think I'll have an egg

The Misfit

There is a man from Trimley Heath
You'll know him by his Rich Brown Teeth
His crooked smile and turned up nose
And the funny way he wears his clothes

His hair looks bad I must confess
It's always in a terrible mess
It looks just like it's been hit by a bomb
I don't think he has a comb

He looks as though he has slept in a gutter
And also has a terrible stutter
He seems to have no luck with ladies
I'm pretty sure he will have no babies

Yet still this man will persist
Although I'm sure he has never been kissed
He looks bad but that's not all
He is only five feet two inches tall

To A Rabbit

I'm proud of you my little rabbit
Although your life is one of habit
And though for years you have been sought
You never yet have been caught

You live in dry land and in bog
Hiding from that pest the dog
Many times I've seen you run
And knew of course t'was not for fun

Among the flowers amidst the trees
Living life the way you please
Having fun with all the ladies
No wonder you have lot's of babies

Your life is full, I must confess
Although no nights of drunkenness
No fights so there's no one to blame
No sense of loss, no sense of shame

Just pure enjoyment every day
Because you live and play that way
One thing more that I might add
I'm sure you love to be a dad.

The Hound of The Baskervilles

In Yorkshire once there lived a hound
Who roamed the moors by night
He gave the most ferocious sound
That everyone took fright

He was a monsterous hairy beast
With ugly gnashing teeth
Saliva dripped with every step
He took upon the heath

His evil eyes, they glowed like fire
A demon in disguise
He killed his victims in the mire
And no-one heard their cries

He stalked his victims with great care
Relying on their spoor
He savaged them and left them there
Dying on the moor

And so for years the legend grew
About this monsterous hound
Who roamed about the moors by night
And made this mournful sound

Then suddenly the killings ceased
No-one could hear his roar
And now they've made this demon beast
The subject of folklore

The Wind and The Sun

There was an argument one day
Between the wind and the sun
The argued long, and had their say
As to who was the stronger one

The wind then said "Do you see the man"?
Now I don't want you to scoff
But he is from the MacDonald clan
And I'll make him take his coat off

Then the wind swooped down, and blew and blew
He blew as hard as he could
But the man held on to his coat like glue
He had great fortitude

At last the wind had had enough
He had tried his very best
But the man below was just too tough
It was the sun's turn to try the test

The sun then beamed upon the ground
The man began to feel quite warm
But he did not even make a sound
He had weathered out the storm

The sun then continued to beam
Until the man got hot
He then removed his coat at last
This was the sun's big plot

The sun then began to smile
The wind was in his debt
For he has used his brain and guile
And had won this foolish bet

34

A Pot of Stew

Now listen to my tale of woe
There are things that you should know
It was on one dark and stormy night
All was black there was no light

At twelve o'clock the hour bewitches
Warlocks goblins and some witches
Sat there stirring a cauldron pot
Boiling a mortal they had caught

Others were dancing and swirling around
All their feet were off the ground
They were all shouting and screaming
I'm very glad I was just dreaming

So hark you now to my tale
When there is a storm or gale
Do not move just sit there tight
And pray to god with all your might

Because if you run they will chase
Until your staring face to face
Then they will cast you in a spell
And make your life a living hell

Then after the pursuit ceases
They will cut you into little pieces
So keep on running don't get caught
Or you'll end up in that cooking pot

But if you leave the status quo
Remember this before you go
When these demons are eating stew
Just make sure the stew's not you

Why the Sparrow is the King of the Birds

The birds all got together one day
To elect the king of the birds
They argued long and had their say
With wise and eloquent words

Until at last they all agreed
With no sign of bias
That the bird who did the special deed
The one who flew the highest

All the birds took flight, and tried their best
There was no use denying
That the eagle went higher than the rest
He was very strong at flying

Up and up the eagle flew
Then he began to tire
He felt his wings were made of glue
Until he could go no higher

Then a strange thing happened, it was weird
He felt something on his back
It was then a little sparrow appeared
He was smarter than a tack

He flew a few feet higher
Than the eagle at his best
He was the highest flyer
And had won the regal test

Then all the birds down below
Began to shout and sing
They took the little sparrow home
And then they made him king

The Meaning of Life

Of all of God's creations
Placed upon this Earth
It's only Man who doesn't know
The reason for his birth

The Dog he has the answer
He's here to bring us joy
He gives his love and is the pet
of every little boy

The Cow he has the knowledge
That we depend on him
He knows we chop him up for food
And sell him limb by limb

The Chicken and the Rooster
Know their importance too
Their here to give us eggs each day
And know they're good for you

The birds and fish would tell you
When we go out to dine
They know they're on the menu
Together with white wine

The Pig of course he knows the most
Which isn't very nice
We use his pork to make a roast
And bacon slice by slice

All the other animals
Know why they're in a Zoo
So naturally are quite content
When we go there to view

But Man with all his knowledge
Has still himself to find
And has this age old question
Forever on his mind

THE THINKER

The Kitten

The winter snow was silent
Tree's had turned to white
The raging wind was violent
As day turned into night

I found a little kitten
Lying frozen in the snow
My foolish heart was smitten
He had no place to go

I took him home that evening
And wrapped him in a shawl
I placed him down beside the fire
And hoped that he would thaw

I'd heard of reincarnation
Discussed it with my wife
So I gave him a drink of gasolene
To bring him back to life

In my heart I knew the truth
There was nothing more I could do
So we all sat down to dinner
And got about halfway through

When all at once the kitten
Jumped from the fireside glow
Then ran around the table
As fast as it could go

The noise it made was scary
It howled, it hissed, it screeched
With our faces pale and wary
You'd think that we'd been bleached

Round and round the table it went
We thought it would never stop
When all of a sudden it's little legs bent
And it fell down with a plop

It lay there silent on it's back
It's legs up in the air
I'm glad it was a kitten
And not a Grizzly Bear

Is it dead; my wife said clearly
No said I alas
I think that it has merely
Just ran out of gas.

PHUT PHUT PHUT

The Apple Tree

The apple tree's rife
It is teeming with life
Above and below the earths surface
The industrious bees
They do as they please
As they buzz around with a purpose

The birds they are fine
And often will dine
Even the old and infirm
But their babies can't fly
And you'll hear them cry
When they want a bug or a worm

Away down below
The worms they don't glow
As they slither silent and mute
It can rain, it can snow
And I'm sure that you know
They don't give a damn or a hoot

And the wise old mole
He sits in his hole
Surveying the sights to be seen
You may think he is crazy
But he isn't lazy
he was wild when he was a teen

So the apple tree stands
The best in the land
Looking so calm and serene
But you cannot deny it
If you think it's quiet
You haven't surveyed the whole scene.

Reflection

Looking in a mirror
I see an old man standing there
This stranger can't be me
I'm still a young man
Experienced perhaps
But the person behind the eyes looking out
The person inside of me
Is still in his youth
But who is this stranger looking at me

I stare at the face of this stranger
Looking for some sign of recognition
But just when I get a glimpse of me
It is gone again
I have changed so much
That even I can't recognize my youthful self
Forever trapped in an aging shell
But I know full well
That the stranger looking at me
IS ME

The Crusades

King Richard he was going to war
To the Holy Land precisely
Saladin and his men were bad
They were not acting nicely

He told his nobles he'd go for a year
And was leaving in the morning
To stay away from Guinevere
It was a royal warning

He must do something else he felt
You may think he was unkind
He fitted the queen with a chastity belt
To give him peace of mind

To Lancelot a round table knight
Who was brave, trustworthy and true
King Richard said I go to fight
But leave the key with you

The morning came, the troops rode out
By noon they were nearing the sea
When from a distance he heard a shout
"King Richard, I've got the wrong key"

Tarzan of The Apes

Lord and lady Greystoke
Were sailing on the sea
One morning just as they awoke
There came catastrophy

It was on the coast of Africa
The ship began to sink
They landed in the ocean
And had no time to think

They swam to the jungle shore
With items that they cherished
The angry sea did rage and roar
The ships crew they all perished

They built a little shanty
To shelter from the wind
It didn't have a pantry
So the food they ate was skinned

Lady Greystoke had a baby boy
The apple of her eye
And though he brought her lot's of joy
The end for her was nigh

The baby was a few weeks old
When the mother died
Lord Greystoke he was in the field
He'd left his gun inside

Along came a killer ape
Who grabbed him by the head
Lord Greystoke he could not escape
And was left lying dead

That only left the little boy
Who was sleeping in his bed
The apes didn't kill him
They took him home instead

Kala was a mother ape
Who was living all alone
She took the infant by the nape
And raised him as her own

The little boy he grew so tall
Until he became a man
He was smarter than them all
they called him Tarzan

Then one day the hairy ape
Who had killed his father dead
Tried to kill young Tarzan
Who hit him back instead

For hours they battled to and fro
The fighting it was fierce
Until Tarzan with a mighty blow
Defences he did pierce

He jumped upon the killer ape
And stabbed him in the heart
The other primates didn't gape
Just pried them both apart

The apes showed no sign of grief
And started eating grapes
Then they made young Tarzan chief
Tarzan of the apes

Absent Minded

In a seniors home there lived a man
Who was getting on in years
He always had an amusing plan
To banish all his fears

One day while shuffling down the hall
He met a lady named Bess
He said to her, how old am I
Come on now, try and guess

She said, if I'm to guess your age
I cannot just assume
I must have something more to gauge
And took him to her room

She told him then to take off his clothes
And leave them on the floor
To turn around and face her
So she could guess the score

She took a long hard look and said
you are eighty two
He was amazed, and said your right
What gave you the clue

Smiling slowly, then she said
This isn't your best day
I guess you don't remember
You told me yesterday

The Salvation Army Band

A salvation army band
Was playing in the street
As they marched along, they sang their song
With a Christian type of beat

They reached the busy village square
A crowd began to throng
The band it formed a circle there
The crowd it sang along

A lady with a tambourine
Began to solicit the crowd
She said hello my name is Jean
And held her head up proud

A slender man who looked ill fed
Put ten dollars on her tray
She was surprised and then she said
what hymn would you like today

The man replied, don't think I'm bold
But I've been drinking rum
And the hymn I'd like, if the truth were told
Is him with the big base drum.

The Thirteenth Hole

Two friends were playing golf one day
When at the thirteenth hole
Mike lined up to make his play
A birdie was his goal

Suddenly to attention he stood
His cap held in his hand
He had a strange, somber mood
John did not understand

Then all at once the reason was clear
A funeral was passing by
And from Mike's eye there came a tear
And from his chest a sigh

John said, Mike I'm truly impressed
You are so full of caring
You stood there sad and so distressed
You have such noble bearing

Mike said thanks, it's the least I could do
As he wiped away the tears
She died at only fifty-two
We were married for twenty years

If Everyone Was Naked

If everyone was naked
I'm sure that we all know
It would be nigh impossible
To tell a friend from foe

The whole wide world would be at peace
With joy throughout the land
There'd be no fights and war's would cease
On every foreign strand

If everyone was naked
From head down to their toes
This world would be a better place
With no one wearing clothes

Crime would stop, streets be safe
No gangs around at night
They would not want to be outside
And feel cold winter's bite

If everyone was naked
And started spouting prose
That would be the only fault
Of no one wearing clothes

The Operation

A woman who was four feet tall
Visited a doctor one day
And said that she would give her all
To make the pain go away

The doctor asked where does it show
She answered "in my loins"
And every time it rains or snows
I get terrible pain in my groins

The doctor then said, don't be sad
Just jump up on this table
I'll have a look at what is bad
And fix it if I'm able

He examined her when she lay prone
And said I'll put you to sleep
When you awake, the pain will be gone
So there's no need to weep

A half hour later she woke up
And said will it be over soon
The doctor replied, drink from this cup
And walk around the room

The pains all gone, the woman cried
And yelled by gee by goshes
What did you do, and he replied
I cut three inches off your Galoshes

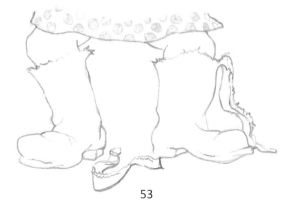

Longevity of Life

A reporter once was asked to write
About longevity of life
he knew about a special site
Called Kelty down in Fife

He traveled down to this small town
And reached the village square
He saw three seniors of renown
Upon a park bench there

He told them that he was a sage
Then asked them to tell their story
Why they had lived to a ripe old age
And their search for fame and glory

The first old man said, I'm only human
There's three things in life that matter
Cigarettes, Liquor and a woman
Especially the latter

I've smoked like a chimney all my life
And I've also drank like a fish
But I've never ever had a wife
I've never had my wish

The reporter said your still alive
Tell me how old are you now
The old man replied he was ninety five
You could tell by his wrinkled up brow

The second old man said, I don't like to dicker
But the same three things still apply
Cigarettes, Women and Liquor
Don't ask me the reason or why

Cigarettes I've smoked them forever
Liquor I drink when I'm dry
But women I've had none, no never
Not even when young and spry

The reporter then asked, how old are you
The old man replied ninety nine
But I'm feeling my age, I can tell you
Comes from drinking all of that wine

The reporter said I'm delighted
And I say that I must confess
You may look little bit blighted
But your age, I would never have guessed

The third old man said, I've had my strife
But I've had a jolly good time
I've smoked cigarettes all of my life
And had many a glass of white wine

Women, I've had by the dozen
So many I've really lost count
But I treated them all quite fairly
And never knocked any about

The reporter then said, you've live a fast track
I would say your were never deprived
How old are you now, and the answer come back
I am thirty-five

The Clockmaker

I've made grandfather clocks
That are seven feet tall
And westminster clocks
That hang on the wall
Clocks that play a beautiful tune
And clocks with cuckoo's that come out at noon

I've made my clocks
With whistles and gauges
And made them strong
To last through the ages
My Clocks will remain of this there's no doubt
For many a year, after I am worn out

I worked all my life
To develop this skill
Though sometimes it felt
Like running uphill
And then when my lathe, it gets rusty and old
My clocks will survive when I'm silent and cold

Now I'm getting old
My life nearly spent
My eyes they grow dim
My back it is bent
I've made my clocks that forever will chime
But I am the one who has run out of time

Imagination

When I am lying on the grass
And cast my eyes up high
To watch the lazy summer clouds
As they go drifting by
Imagination knows no bounds
And clouds become most things
Like motor cars and pirate ships
And even diamond rings

The Argument

Two men were having an argument one day
Both men they liked to boast
They argued long and had their say
On who could see the most

The one eyed man said I'm like you
Although I have one eye
I see the very same as you
And all the things you try

I see the flowers, I see the trees
The mountains and the river
I even see a chicken sneeze
And rabbits all a quiver

But one thing more, it's no surprise
We know when things are done
I can see your two eyes
You can only see my one

The Duck

A lady once went to a store
With a pet duck under her arm
She carried him around the floor
To keep him out of harm

She saw a salesman at a table
Wearing long black hair
He was writing something on a label
And just ignored the pair

She said to him, you make me nervous
Just get off your butt
I want some instant service
Don't sit there like a nut

The man looked up, then he said
Is that pig with you
She replied, your off your head
You haven't got a clue

You must be as blind as a bat
It's not a pig, It's a duck
The salesman replied, I know that
I was talking to the duck

Loyalty

Companies have a reputation
That they favour separation
No. not the Province of Quebec
It's staff that get it in the neck

It's to these staff that I refer
Who spend a lifetime working there
Some work for thirty years or more
At sixty they are shown the door

That's the way it's been for years
They do not care, when age appears
The staff don't really have a say
They're let go with one year's pay

The mood is bad with what goes on
Staff feel that they are put upon
Of course they're scared to have their say
They know that they'll be chopped one day

Loyalty's like a two edged sword
That companies had in plenty
But now the way they treat their staff
The barrel's almost empty

In The Garden

We sat in the garden
Enjoying the daylight
Remembering how things used to be
We sat for a while
You gave me a smile
When I put my hand on your knee

We remembered back when
Men had to be men
I carved our names on a tree
But you got a fright
That terrible night
When I put my hand on your knee

You said I was bad
A horrible cad
I guess that it had to be me
I was to blame
For that unthinkable shame
When I put my hand on your knee

The years they went past
'Till one day at last
Instead of wanting to flee
You took my hand
You must understand
And placed it right there on your knee

A Fisherman of Men

In the Sherway Store there works a man
Bruno Puppo is his name
He does his job with great elan
Fishing is his game

He is like the lord above
A fisherman of men
But instead of giving them his love
He puts them in the Penn.

The selling floor is Bruno's pond
The customers are like fish
He'll wait and watch till they abscond
With any little dish

As store detective he won't flinch
Until the people steal
Then he pulls them in like fish
Although he has no reel

He has a very active mind
And takes the time to think
He knows that they will rob you blind
As quick as you can blink

For Bruno, yes' this job is right
When on the selling floor
He'll wait until the thieves do bite
Then catch them at the door

So listen Lord and hear his prayer
Let him sing and shout
Let him catch a thief that's rare
One he can boast about

Fuddle Duddle

Pierre Trudeau says Fuddle Duddle
When he's in a tight spot or two
But we know when he says Fuddle Duddle
He really means God Bless You

Now we know he loves all the workers
We should cause he gives us this clue
Everytime that he says Fuddle Duddle
We know it means God Bless You

Ed. Broadbent is not in the picture
He can't be with his part-time crew
But we know if he were the Prime Minister
He'd say Fuddle Duddle too

Mulrooney say's he'll save the nation
If we give him the mandate to do
But we know he wont say Fuddle Duddle
Instead he'll say go screw you.

The Eulogy

John Doe passed away this morning
He lived an active life
He went without a warning
And very little strife

He was a friendly fellow
Though when young a little wild
But in later years did mellow
And was kind to every child

Be sad a while don't grieve too much
John's in a better place
He suffered yes, but in the clutch
A smile was on his face

Think of him up there in heaven
No taxes to defray
He has the frills without the bills
And has no rent to pay

So if you have to shed a tear
Do so without misgiving
Remember though, the dead don't care
So shed them for the living

HARVEY & HOLLY

EVE   OSCAR   FLO

ARCHIE   BRACKEN

The Dachshund Man

I have a friend a Kelty man
John Whitelaw is his name
He breeds dogs with great elan
Dachshunds bring hint fame

Their legs are short just like pegs
Have long and droopy ears
But when they sit up and beg
Are cute and cuddly dears

Although they are small when in a race
Can outrun a spaniel
They have lots of speed and grace
According to the manual

Germans used them to hunt
Thought they were heaven sent
Because when born and still a runt
Were so intelligent

They will chew most things in sight
Are small and smooth haired
They will very seldom fight
No matter how alley are reared

They are also very loyal
Their life span fourteen years
Queen Victoria made them royal
Her dachshunds had no peers

When they are fully grown
Are eight to ten inches high
They will clave a brownish tone
That is the time to buy

So if you want to buy a hound
And money you must spend
Don't get a dog from the pound
Buy a dachshund from my friend

Andrew Carnegie

Andrew Carnegie a clever Scottish man
Dunfermline was the place where it all began
He went to America while in his youth
The story that I tell you is the honest truth

He was born in Dunfermline
In a house on Moodie Street
Andrew had lots of kin
As nice as you could meet

The custom that was old and true
In fact it was not bad
They christened him Andrew
In honour of his grandad

Andrew was a self made man
Now his story can be told
He made money with great elan
By being brave and bold

He did not even go to school
Until the age of eight
But Andrew he was not a fool
Although he started late

At thirteen years old he emigrated
To Pitsburgh the destination
Because of all the smoke and grime
Was the dirtiest in the nation

He was offered a job he did not seek
And became a telegraph boy
Was paid two dollars and fifty cents a week
It brought him lots of joy

He worked hard never quit
Being lazy was not his style
And when a friend needed help a bit
Would go that extra mile

His name was Carnegie
He did not have a fault
When he received his pay
He put it in a vault

He received a worthwhile tip
From a man who invented steel
They went into partnership
Shook hands to sign the deal

To the railroad he sold bridges and rails
Which were stronger than they had
That is how he made lots of sales
Although he was still a lad

He partnered a man named Pulman
Who designed a sleeping van
He sold it as a railroad car
For people who travelled far

Over the years he bought shares
In companies old and new
Success will come to those who dare
These shares just grew and grew

Then when he decided to retire
He sold every company on his list
And when he had no irons in the fire
He became a philanthropist

He donated over three thousand libraries
Had thousands of callers
Gave it to charities, hospitals and friends of his
Three hundred and fifty million dollars

And yet despite an early rift
With Pittencrieff and its glade
Dunfermline glens the most satisfying gift
That he ever made

Now you've heard the story
And his life has been unfurled
Although it was never gory
He became the richest man in the world

LOVE VERSES

LOVE

When you fall in love the first time
It is an accident
When you fall in love the second time
It is a coincidence
When you fall in love a third time
It's your own fault.

The Cure for LOVE

there are so many kinds of love
Some lustful and some pure
And many loves will last for years
Before they find the cure

The cure is there for all to see
But we don't realize
For being mortal we can't see
What's right before our eyes

I grant you this the cures not small
And requires a lot of courage
But I will tell you, one and all
The cure for love is marriage.

Five Kinds of LOVE

Five kinds of love
Have existed since time began
The first it is a peaceful love
That's in the heart of man

It's the love you give your mother
And friendships you've pursued
It makes every man a brother
It's strong although subdued

The second love is from the waist
And not a love to trust
It often comes with too much haste
We sometimes call it lust

The third combines the love from heart
With love that's from the waist
And that is how romance start
And marriage are based

The fourth love it is so divined
Beneath the setting sun
It is a love that's from the mind
And not for everyone

It is a love that drives men mad
And lures them to their doom
The strangest love we've ever had
The kind that will consume

The fifth love is the perfect love
From heart, the waist, the mind
But it is the elusive love
Most people never find

So if you fall in love one day
And want some peace of mind
Just remember that
Five kinds of love exist for all mankind

MAE

You are my wife
You are my life
The essence of my soul
As I grow old and fall apart
Your love will keep me whole

There are times
It seems my dear
We appear to grow apart
But whether we are far or near
I hold you in my heart

Remember

Do you remember the night we wed
Do you remember the words we said
We vowed our love throughout the years
To keep it strong through toil and tears
Do you remember? Do you remember?
How you used to hold your hand in mine
If you remember, like I remember
Our love will last through time

I know it's late now, the years have passed
We have contentment, here at last
The memories that I share with you
The story of a love that grew
So please remember, yes please remember
To be happy when I've gone away
If you remember, like I remember
Our love is here to stay

I'll always love you and I know
That you will miss me when I go
So please remember what I say
And do not throw your life away
And when I'm gone dear, your must be strong dear
Cause you'll have to live your life for me
And please remember, like I remember
Of how we used to be

I'll Write A Lovesong To You Dear

We've loved each other for a long time
Ever since we met
We've loved each other for a long time
With never a regret
I've never told you all my feelings
I've never said how much I care
We'll love each other for a lifetime
And have a lovely affair

I'll write a lovesong to you dear
To tell you all the words you want to hear
How all the little things you do for me
Just tend to let me see
How much you mean to me (dear)
I'll write a sonnet to my love
And sprinkle it with stars from up above
Forgive my transgresses
And return my caresses
If you love me my dear

Your love is like a breeze in spring
It's like a warm embrace
My heart it feels it wants to sing
A song in your praise
I think that you are so appealing
I love you more and more each day
Your love can send my senses reeling
In every kind of way

I know that I'd be lost without you
Lost without your smile
You have that certain thing about you
That air of grace and style
I know that you're a real good dancer
And through this life our footsteps we will blend
I think I've found the perfect answer
A love that never will end

I Had A Dream Last Night

I had a dream last night
We dined by the candlelight
The air filled with your perfume
There was magic in the room
With gold shining in your hair
My heart told me to beware
We started to dance
You gave me romance
And I had no chance my dear
Cause right from the start
I lost my heart
When I had a dream last night

I had a dream last night
We danced in the pale moonlight
The stars that were in your eyes
Gave a glimpse of paradise
I held you close in my arms
My heart was a slave to your charms
When love is in bloom
It's safe to assume
That love will consume my dear
Cause right from the start
I lost my heart
When I had a dream last night

I'm Sentimental

I'm sentimental when I think of you
I'm sentimental of things we used to do
I feel a sadness because we had to part
But when I'm sentimental you're here in my heart

I remember times when grass was green
Of the many happy years you were my queen
I remember times when skies were blue
I know it's because I loved you

I'll love you forever till the day I die
I'll love you forever although I seldom cry
I feel so lonely since you went away
But by loving you forever you're in my heart to stay

I remember birds sing in the trees
Of lovely flowers dancing, in the breeze
I remember rainbows golden hue
I know it's because I love you

I know you loved me more than life can tell
I know you loved me and I love you as well
I know you wouldn't like it, to see me sad this way
So I'll try to be happy and show my love that way

Now I will wipe the tear drops from my eyes
And look up at the blue that's in the sky
I'll listen to the little birds that sing
And accept, what this life may bring

Jack and Isa

Jack is the nicest man
That I really know
I think that he is perfect
From head down to his toe

I've never met a person
That he did not like
Although he was mischievous
When just a little tyke

His loyalty is like no other
And never will it bend
I'm glad he is my brother
And also my best friend

He has a very lovely wife
She is a classy dame
And just like jack was born in fife
Isa is her name

Isa does the household chores
And never gets irate
Because when cleaning all the floors
Gets help from her mate

Our loving parents gave us growth
And a worldly start
So when I say I love you both
I mean it from my heart

A Rose

A rose is a beautiful flower
The symbol of true love
And though from an earthly bower
It seems from heaven above

It is like loves old sweet song
Until it withers and dies
But when in bloom can do no wrong
And poets idolize

A rose signifies many things
Just like a pure white dove
Wedding bands and diamond rings
When they are given with love

A Special thing

Love is a feeling
Sometimes it is unkind
It can send your senses reeling
They say that love is blind

Love has so many faces
Can make you lose your pride
It puts you through your paces
You'll wish that you had died

Unrequited love is the worst
It makes you go through hell
Until your heart is ready to burst
A feeling you can't quell

But when you love someone that's true
Although you may have faults
If that love returns to you
Your heart it exhaults

Love is a very special thing
With it you cannot measure
But when it makes your heart sing
Treat it like a treasure

Honky Tonk Woman

Out in the West
Where the stars shine so bright
I lost my heart
In a dance hall one night
She wore a gown
That was crimson and white
And I fell in love with Sadie

She smiled at me
As she came down the stair
She was the girl
With gold in her hair
I tried to be
So debonaire
That's when I met my lady

I looked at her
And I saw at a glance
That she liked me
And she wanted to dance
We both found love
And we welcomed romance
Though both our pasts were shady

She's a honky tonk woman
And she is my friend
She'll stand beside me
Right through to the end
And now that my wandering
Is over and done
With my honky tonk woman, I'll have some fun

An Old Fashioned Christmas

Let us have an old fashioned Christmas
With the family
Let us have some fun and some laughter
Gathered round the tree
You will find that all hearts will be brighter
Than the Christmas snow
And you will find your spirits will be lighter
Everywhere you go

Let's all have a Merry Merry Christmas
With presents neath the tree
We'll have fun with everybody singing
Oh so merrily
You will hear the church bells ring
And listen to the choir sing
There will be safe piece of mind
With sweet harmony

Let us have an old fashioned Christmas
By the fireside glow
Kissing all your friends, and your loved ones
Neath the mistletoe
You will find that fun is in the giving
When snow is on the ground
And you will find a better way of living
When love is all around

Let us make our old fashioned Christmas
A time for tears of joy
And make sure that all of the children
Get a Christmas toy
You will find when everyone is sleeping
Santa will appear
And let's hope the magic of the moment
Spreads throughout the year

My Grandson

Kellen is little boy
Who is only five years old
But oh' he brings my life such joy
It's lovely to behold

Each time he enters in a room
It is a wonderous sight
He scatters all the doom and gloom
The world seems warm and bright

He likes to hear a story
About the days of old
How knights would fight for glory
By being brave and bold

It 's nice to share a love so young
With no reservations
That is why we have such fun
Though different generations

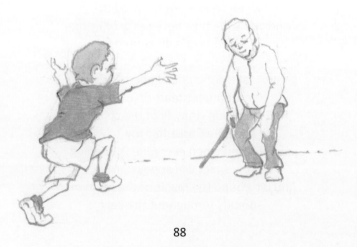

An Honourable Man

Allan Craig is an honourable man
A wise and noble sage
A member of the McKinnon clan
Of Scottish heritage

His tartan heart is staunch and true
The bluebell is his flower
For Scotland's sake he'll drink a few
On any day or hour

He'll always help his fellowman
No matter what the call
He does it well with proud elan
This Scotsman, he stands tall

Though many years have come and gone
And now his hair is white
Give him his due, he soldiers on
He's still a leading light

Archie

The Die was cast
Away back when
As children
We were young again

We are brother and sister
You and I
Two distant stars
In a frightened sky

Although each played
Quite different roles
We are Humans each
With kindred souls

We knew each once
Then drifted apart
Yet still you never
Left my heart

So Archie
You must hear me say
I've always loved you
Your sister
Mae.

Colin Morrison

Colin is a Policeman
Of this there is no doubt
He is quietly spoken
I have never heard him shout

He has the cutest son
And a beautiful spouse
They all live in Dunfermline
In a lovely house

He will stop a car in fife
That is speeding over the limit
Especially when there is a wife
And children sitting in it

There are thieves who steal with care
So let him sing and shout
Let him catch a crook that's rare
One he can boast about

The Love Affair

There was night when at a dance
We fell in love at first glance
I really liked your shape and style
Then we sat down for a while

Each time I looked upon your face
It never failed my heart would race
There were times you were not kind
But I always had you on my mind

Our love affair has lasted well
Though there were times I went through hell
Sometimes I thought I was insane
Because you brought me so much pain

But now I think I had my fill
You were always an expensive bill
So no more money no more tax
It's time I started to relax

Our love affair has lasted long
And through the years it has been strong
But I'm letting you go with no regret
You damned elusive cigarette

100 Years Old

Aunt Betty, you are young and hale
Although one hundred years old,
I know your body may be frail
But your heart is as good as gold.

It's true you are a little slower
And your hair has shades of white,
but one thing more you cannot ignore
You are still a lovely sight.

In conversations you never quit,
Have a clever and active mind,
When you talk you are quite a wit,
A type that's hard to find.

Now you have reached one hundred years
But it's time only marked with a pen,
I'm sure you will banish all doubts and fears
And start life all over again.

So when I say I love you
Though we are far apart,
Just enjoy a life that's new,
I mean it from my heart.

The Greatest Sight I've Ever Seen

I have seen some lovely sights
A rose without a thorn
I have seen a baby lamb
Before its fleece was shorn
I've seen the pure white driven snow
Fall on a wintry morn
But the greatest sight I've ever seen
Was my child when she was born

I've seen the mist upon the brae
The heather in full bloom
I have seen a butterfly
Emerge from its cocoon
In my mind's eye I've even seen
The fabled unicorn
But the greatest sight I've ever seen
Was my child when she was born

I've seen daVinci's masterpiece
The mona Lisa's smile
I have seen a blushing bride
As she came down the aisle
I've seen a country garden wall
And the flowers that there adorn
But the greatest sight I've ever seen
Was my child when she was born

I have seen some lovely sights
A maiden all forlorn
I have travelled far and wide
And seen the Matterhorn
I've seen the mighty oak that grew
From just a small acorn
But the greatest sight I've seen
Was my child when she was born

And if I were Methuselah
And lived a thousand years
The saddest sight I'd ever see
Would be my daughters tears

Kelty

Kelty is a fair size town
That flowers and tree's adorn
The perfect jewel in Scotland's crown
The place where I was born

There's a splendid view of Benarty Hill
Where sheep go there to graze
And I can see the heather still
On lovely summer days

The borderline is the black burn
It divides Kinross from Fife
A place where I had lot's of fun
When in my younger life

The Aitken Pit the Lindsay
The Blair and Bathie too
These pit's were all forsaken
And have vanished from our view

And when I walk up Stewarts Brae
To reach the Kelty Cross
I notice that the Co-op has gone
It is Kelty's loss

The people there are friendly
They greet you with a smile
And if they think you need their help
Will go that extra mile

And though I left this country base
To get my worldly start
I will have special place
For Kelty in my heart

XXX

The Beauty Queen

She was a beautiful woman
And the mother of four
Although she was a human
Was a person you couldn't ignore.

She was five foot eight inches tall
Her hair like natural spun gold
In truth she was a living doll
Just lovely to behold.

She was blonde with shoulder-length hair
Her beauty was unsurpassed
Men would always stop and stare
Turn their heads as she walked past.

She had a nice speaking voice
And stood out in a crowd
She also walked with grace and poise
With her head up straight and proud.

She had three daughters and a son
They were born in fife
She gave them care with lots of fun
Made sure they had a good life.

She loved harvey a miniture dog
He was as light as a feather
They would always go for a walk
No matter what kind of weather.

She liked to tour the highlands
Worked on a submarine
Loved to hear the pipe bands
Met the shop steward's wife, christine.

In the mornings she would hoover the house
And never did complain
She wouldn't even grouse
Just hoover it at night again.

She worked as a wool spinner
A demanding occupation
Again she was a winner
With great determination.

She entered a beauty contest
And had no fear of loss
Though at times she was hard pressed
Won the title of miss kinross.

God works in a mysterious way
I guess he wants the best
He always makes the good ones pay
And took her to his vest

Grandchildren she had seven
Her praises they have sung
She has now gone to heaven
For only the good die young

LIFE VERSES

Cry No Tears

When I am gone don't cry for me
My spirits loose, my soul is free
I made mistakes in great detail
My mind was strong, my body frail
I lived my life to some extent
So please, no tears, and no lament

The Dancing Flowers

One day as I walked along a lonely lane
I saw some flowers that shook their heads and danced
So happy, lively and immune to pain
As though they wanted me to take a chance

I wondered if they had some thoughts
As I went passing by
Of foreign lands and fancy yachts
Instead of where they lie

There's times I'm sure they must feel sad
Not knowing of their fate
They do not know they will enjoy
A boy on his first date

They make us smile at happy times
And even sad times too
They brighten up the whole wide world
When it's feeling blue

So when I walk that lonely lane
And while away the hours
To ease the problem in my brain
I stop and smell the flowers

LIFE

Life is like a river's tears
Just one continuous flow
We work so hard for many years
With little left to show

We put things off or so it seems
The things we should have done
Our life is left with broken dreams
Instead of having fun

So listen now, take my advice
This world is not forgiving
Forget the cost, forget the price
It's time we did some living

Life is just too precious
To waste these golden hours
So please take time and don't forget
To stop and smell the flowers

HOPE

In the deep dark days and sorrowful nights
When life is at it's worst
When all you feel is hunger
And you have unslakable thirst

When all your thoughts are torment
And you feel you want to die
It's the hope that lies there dormant
That gives the need to try

It is lifes sweetest treasure
That plays a merry tune
With it you cannot measure
No-one is quite immune

For hope will lift your spirits up
You'll start your life anew
And you will drink from nectars cup
Before your life is through

Changing Values

Sometimes I think the World' gone mad
And lost it's dignity
What happened to the good and bad
And sense of chivalry

There was a time, when bad was black
And good was always white
We always knew the front and back
The World was warm and bright

Now life has changed, we've lost the old Guard
Like the Sun as it sinks in the west
And each passing year, it really gets hard
To know what to do for the best

Our values have eroded
Why I'm not quite sure
But I remember better days
When the world was young and pure

But don't give up, there's more to come
Hold your banner high and unfurled
Perhaps when it's over, and all is done
We will have a better World

Things To Remember

The glory of the dawn
When grass is wet with dew
The beauty of the setting sun
When daylight hours are through
The joy of a baby
When taking it's first step
The emotion of a first love
The feeling and the depth

The comfort of mother
Who holds you close and sings
The romance before the marriage
And happiness it brings
The lovely tender moment
That comes with your first kiss
Remember these special times
That bring you so much bliss

The names of two young lovers
Carved upon a tree
The wonderment of Santa
When your only three
The beauty of a painting
When it's done in style
Remember these and you will find
Your life will be worthwhile

Reminiscing

We reminisce about the past
A life that might have been
Love affairs that did not last
Places never seen

Listening to the voices
Foundations to be laid
Life is full of choices
Decisions to be made

So when we look back yonder
And try to second guess
Is it any wonder
Our mind is so distressed

Growing Old

When young, our life was full of hope
Ambitions they were high
The world was ours to conquer
As soon as we could fly

We were loved, we were adored
Our parents loving foil
Like eagles in the sky we soared
Above lifes mundane toil

We were strong so full of life
And lived life to the full
There never was a moments strife
Although we bent the rule

The eagle's cry is softer now
We do not fly so high
We'll be content' that is a vow
When time of death draws nigh

Silently Falling

The cold void of darkness
Enclosed my body
As I fell
The engines silent now
My seat melted away
And I fell
Spinning effortlessly
Like a satin doll
Into the quietness of blue sky
Wraith like shapes of different sizes
Mute and silent
Fell with me
As I passed through a white cloud
I knew my spiral
Could only end one way
I had no time to weep
Or be afraid
Down Down
Silently falling
Towards death
And the unknown.

Hate

Have you ever hated anyone
Fiercely with a passion
Like when we have to go to war
And hate it is in fashion

We hate the enemy the foe
And think we have a reason
For it's the only way to go
When hatred is in season

There is another type of hate
A hate that's for your neighbour
The person who is always late
And now is out of favour

There is the kind of hate of course
That is often called dislike
It is strong and is a force
When told to take a hike

Love and hate go together
Both are a strong emotion
But they are difficult to measure
When they are set in motion

So if you hate someone or thing
Resentments you have built
To life's values you must cling
And live life to the hilt

Snowflakes

Snowflakes twinkle in the sky
As they fall from heaven to earth
They came down from that place on high
At the time of our Saviours birth

They give this world a silent grace
And arrive when winters here
They put a smile on every face
That lasts throughout the year

They are lighter than a feather
And are a wonderful sight
When they are packed together
We can have a snowball fight

So when I wake on Christmas morn
And see the kids at play
I'm glad that our Lord was born
Way back on Christmas day

Charity

Charity begins at home
It means it's for yourself
Especially if you tend to roam
And have no power or pelf

But if you have something to give
Then give it from the heart
For it will help someone live
And give them a new start

Then I'm sure that you will find
That love is in full bloom
You will have such peace of mind
That shatters doom and gloom

For when you give I'm sure you know
Love flows just like a river
It drives away all cares and woe
And benefits the giver

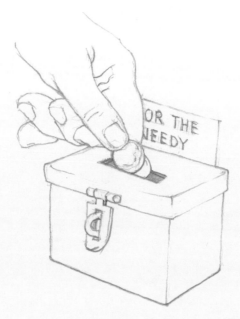

Birds

When I awake each morning
Amid the sunlight's glow
I hear a bird that's singing
Its voice is sweet and low

Birds are a beautiful sight
As they fly from tree to tree
And often they will sing in flight
They were born to be free

So when they're soaring in the sky
And I hear their wonderful sound
I sometimes wonder why I can't fly
As I'm lying on the ground

But I know creatures large and small
All have something to give
And I feel sure when I hear their call
That's why they are born to live

When We Go To Sleep

We die a little every night
When we go to sleep
All our cares are out of sight
If that sleep is deep

But if we don't wake up one morn
And we are found there dead
Gabriel can blow his horn
At least we are in our bed

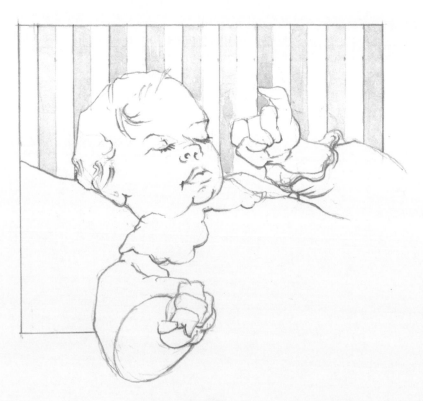

The Measure of a Man

If there lives a man over seventy five
Who doesn't feel lucky to be alive
Born in wedlock has had little strife
And overall had a wonderful life

Despite his assets this ungrateful man
Should change his habits while he can
Stop his boasting and telling lies
And do it soon before he dies

He should not think of money or fame
But concentrate on from whence he came
To go back to the very beginning
Of his childhood days and solid upbringing

If he doesn't change soon you will hear him yell
On judgement day as he goes to hell
For the measure of a man when he is dying
Is the number of friends who stand there crying

The Egg

An egg it is the perfect food
It has an oval shape
It's smaller than an orange
And larger than a grape

They make a tasty omelette
Boil them if you will
And then on Easter Sunday
You can roll them down a hill

They will make you healthy
And also make you wise
They can make you wealthy
By selling them in pies

Fried, poached or scrambled
You can even feed a dog
But the best way is to make a drink
A punch they call eggnog

The Golden Years

They say these are the Golden Years
As portrayed in poem and song
But just when one problem clears
Another one comes along

Each year as we got older
And have all kinds of woes
Our problems just get bolder
And keeps us on our toes

When young our shapely figure
Was always very slim
But now its grown much bigger
We're no longer neat and trim

But poets and songwriters
Don't care if we should cry
The scoundrels and the blighters
Still write this big white lie

A Happy New Year

Come along, sing along, join in the fun
Let's have a happy new year
Come along, you belong, meet every one
Raise your voice loud and clear
Circulate, celebrate, we've just begun
New you can hear the crowd cheer
Stand up and shout it, no doubt about it
We'll have a happy new year

Lets us drink a toast to every one
Here's to yours and mine
And we'll have a drink or two tonight
For the sake of auld Lang Syne

Come along, sing along, join in the fun
Let's have a happy new year
Come along, you belong, meet every one
Raise your glass drink your beer
Circulate, celebrate we've just begun
Now you can hear the crowd cheer
Stand up and shout it, no doubt about it
We'll have a happy new year

The Bottle of Whiskey

One of my favourite stories that my father told me was about The Bottle of Whiskey.

Mrs. Brogan was a big Irish woman who owned a little sweetie shop on the corner of our tenement building called Adams Terrace. She had converted part of her living room into a small sweetie shop, and all the kids in the neighbourhood used to buy their candies from her. They did so because of one reason, Mrs. Brogan was nearly always drunk and was very careless where she put her money. The cash till was just a small drawer located beside the candy and invariably because she was nearly always drunk, some money would find itself among the candies. It was not unusual for a kid to go in for a quarter pound of candies and later find some money among them. Anyway, one day she ran out of whiskey. So she came out of her shop and shouted to my uncle Owen who was playing across the field with some other boys, Owen; Owen; she shouted until my uncle Owen who was just a small boy at the time, came running over to her, to see what she wanted. Owen she said I would like you to run up to McBains and get me a bottle of whiskey, here's the money. Owen dutifully ran up to McBains which was a licensed grocery shop, purchased a bottle of whiskey and promptly returned to Mrs. Brogan with the whiskey. Mrs. Brogan gave him a tip for running the errand. A few days later, Mrs. Brogan again sent him up to McBains for another bottle of whiskey. This time however some of his pals went with him and they were prepared. They went up to McBains purchased a bottle of whiskey, then poured half of it into an empty bottle that they had acquired. They then filled both bottles up with water, secured the tops, and returned to Mrs. Brogan, to whom they promptly gave one bottle of whiskey. Mrs Brogan as I said before, was nearly always drunk, so she never knew that the whiskey had been watered down. A few days later she again called Owen, and sent him for a bottle of whiskey. He made the pretense of going up to McBains, then promptly gave her the second bottle of whiskey that had been watered down. It was her own whiskey, but she never knew it, this went on for a very long time, almost every second day. I haven't taken the time to calculate how much whiskey, or should I say money, for her own whiskey, that they took from her. And she never did ever know that she had been taken.

Playing Hooky

When my uncle Eddy was a boy, he got into the habit of playing hooky from school.

His timing was not very good however, because one day when he was playing hooky, the school sent a representative to my grandmothers house. When he asked for Eddy, my grandmother said he's at school. The representative then told my grandmother that he was not at school, and told her the number of times, he had been missing from school.

Now Eddy was having a great time. He was in the co-operative bakery where all the goodies were being made. When it was time for him to go home, he methodically brushed all the flour off his clothes. When he was spick and span, he went off home, where his mother was waiting for him. His mother said, where have you been Eddy, to which he replied; Oh! I've been to school all day. His mother was beginning to wonder what was going on. Had the school made a mistake, she was puzzled about it, until Eddy turned away to go to his room. The back of his clothes were white with flour dust. He had cleaned the front of his clothes alright, but had forgotten to clean the back of them, needless to say Eddie did not sit down for about a week

THE STONE BRIDGE

The Stone Bridge

Kelty is a fair size town, and at one end of Kelty there is a small river that is the borderline between the counties of Fifeshire and Kinrosshire.

A road runs over the River, so naturally there is a small stone bridge that spans the river. This was the scene when my father, Alex Duffy, and a few of his pals arrived there. Being only small boys at the time, they decided to do a little mischief. The Bridge being quite old, was not too sturdy, so they proceeded to push the stones into the water, when they had finished pushing the stones into the river, they decided that they had had enough, and went on their way to do something else. Unknown to them however, one of the cottagers who lived nearby saw them, and recognizing a few of them, notified the police. They were charged with vandalism and had to go to court. The judge read out the charge. And when he was finished, he said to my father, what do you have to say for yourself. My father said, well your honour, my friends and I did push over the sides of the bridge, but we did it because we were afraid that someone would get hurt or killed. Every week courting couples come and lean on the sides of the bridge, and we were afraid that something terrible might happen to them, so we pushed the sides of the bridge into the water so that no one would get hurt. You must admit your honour, that if we small boys could push it over into the river, it must have been very bad indeed. The judge contemplated for a few moments then said, case dismissed.

Keeping Up

It's not easy growing old. You try to keep your mind alert, The way you always used to, but your body tires and your Legs start to ache, and sometimes you cannot be bothered. Doing things you once thought to be exciting. Issues you once thought to be important, don't seem to matter Any more.

Life, especially in business, is moving at a faster pace and you find it increasingly difficult to keep up. Retirement or the thought of it, which you once dreaded, doesn't seem too bad anymore.

The big problem, is that no-one, not even your wife will let you grow old gracefully and let you feel your age.

In business, you are expected to keep up with the young eager beavers who will work long hours and will do anything to get ahead. Mentally you have to be on your toes every minute of the day. You cannot let up or you will be engulfed with paperwork which is rushing to you with ever increasing speed and quantity. You get home each night, mentally and physically exhausted, but you know your wife doesn't want to live with a tired old man, so you try to do things you think will please her. You try your best, but you know that without a rest, you will not be able to continue. So you have a nap to refresh yourself. This too however, become a big problem, because you wife, not knowing the state of exhaustion your in, thinks that you are being lazy and acting like an old man. What she fails to realize is that you are an old man who needs a rest.
Sometimes it feels that the only way to slow things down is to be sick, break a leg, or contract a rare tropical disease. As I said before, no-one will let you grow old gracefully. You are constantly being pushed to the limit.

When you were younger, you looked forward to your day off so that you could play golf or tennis. Now you look forward to a day of rest.

There is one consolation however. From time to time you hear things and notice that other people at work are having trouble coping too. In fact, they being less experienced than you, seem to be even worse off in keeping up. You say to yourself, I'm glad it isn't only me who is feeling the pressure and it's not because of age. No it's because life is actually changing at a faster pace.

The Handicap

Three men and a woman went to play golf one day.

They reached the 1st hole, Arthur teed up and hit his ball into the woods on the left. The girl started to laugh, please don't laugh said Arthur, I have a handicap. What's your handicap said the girl. I have a wooden arm said Arthur, I don't believe you, said the girl, show me, so Arthur unscrewed his wooden arm and showed it to her. I would never have believed that she said, I saw you walking down from the clubhouse swinging your arms, you looked so natural.

The 2nd man James teed up his ball and hit it out of the bounds to the right. Again the girl started to laugh. Please don't laugh said James, I have a handicap too. What's your handicap said the girl. James said, I have a wooden leg, I don't believe you, said the girl. So James unscrewed his wooden leg and showed it to her, I would never have believed that said the girl. I watched you walk down here from the Clubhouse, you looked so natural.

The 3rd man John teed up his ball and swung. He topped his ball and it only went about ten yards. The girl started to laugh again. Please don't laugh said John I have a handicap too. what's your handicap the girl said in disbelief. I have a wooden head said John. Now that I don't believe said the girl, nobody has a wooden head. I am telling you I have a wooden head said John. You didn't believe Arthur when he said he had a wooden arm. You didn't believe James when he said he had a wooden leg. Now you don't believe me. When I tell you that I have a wooden head. Ok said the girl this is ridiculous but show me your wooden head not here said John its too embarrassing, wait till we get back to the clubhouse.

The foursome then finished the 18 holes of golf and returned to the clubhouse.

They were sitting at a table having a drink when the girl said to John, you were going to show me your wooden head. John said not here it's too embarrassing lets go to the locker room.

About twenty minutes passed and Arthur said to James. They've been gone along time I wonder what has happened to them. I'll have a look to see if I can find them. He got up and made his way to the locker room, and as he opened the locker room door, there was John and the girl, John was screwing his head off.

The Undertaker

Johnny Mathews was the manager of the Kelty Cooperative Joinery Dept. As manager he also did double duty as the local undertaker.

One day he received a telephone call from Mrs. Brown who said she needed his services as an undertaker. It seemed that her husband had died. Mrs. Brown lived down at the bottom end of Kelty. Johnny promptly made a call on her. When he reached the house, he knocked on the door, and Mrs. Brown answered the door. Johnny said I'm sorry about your loss Mrs. Brown and I have brought a shroud for your husband. Mrs. Brown said, I am very sorry Johnny, but he hasn't quite gone yet. Could you go for a walk for twenty minutes. I'm sure he will be gone by then, so Johnny always obliging went for a half hour walk. When he returned, Mrs. Brown said Johnny I am sorry about this but he still hasn't gone. Could you take another walk. I'm sure he will be gone when you return. Johnny once again went for a walk. This time he took an hour. When he returned the second time, Mrs Brown said, I can't understand it Johnny but he still hasn't gone, could you go for another walk. By this time Johnny had had enough. So he said to Mrs. Brown. I'll tell you what, you take the shroud and when your husband does pass away, you give me a call and I'll come down as fast as I can. Mrs. Brown took the shroud and said she would do just that. About three weeks later Johnny was having breakfast in his home, when someone knocked on his door. When Johnny went to answer the door, he found a man standing there. The man said, Johnny, I'm Mr. Brown and I am returning the shroud. I didn't need it after all.

A Shaggy Dog Story

John was walking along the beach one day and he found a Rary, which had been washed ashore.

He was very excited about this and decided to take it home. However, his wife took one look at it and said get that thing out of here, I can't stand to look at it. So John thought I'll give it to my friend Arthur. However, when Arthur saw it, he said, I don't want it, I don't even like it.

So John then traveled to Edinburgh, where he tried to give it away, but nobody wanted it. He tried Glasgow, Motherwell, Dunfermline and even Kelty, but with the same result, nobody wanted it.

He then traveled down to London yet still nobody wanted it. He then thought about New York and how they were very open minded about things. So he went to New York but had the same result, nobody wanted it. He tried several cities in Canada, including Toronto and Winnipeg, still with the same result, nobody wanted the Rary.

He then tried Paris, France, Germany, Poland and other European countries but still nobody wanted the Rary.

By this time, he had given up hope, of anyone wanting the Rary. He finally decided to go back to Scotland.

He then climbed Ben Nevis, the highest mountain in Scotland. When he arrived at the top, he looked over the side and noticed that there was a sheer drop, all the way down. He took the Rary and threw it over the side. He then said boy! That was a long way to tip a Rary.

The Proposal

Two friends, John and Arthur were at a dance one night. They both asked girls up to dance. When the dance finished, John went over to their table and sat down. Arthur was still on the dance floor talking to the girl. John watched them for a few minutes, when the girl took her hand and slapped Arthur across the face. His face turned a bright red. When Arthur came back and sat down beside him, John said, what did you say to that girl, that made her slap you like that. Arthur replied. Oh I just asked her if she wanted to come to my place and have some passionate sex. John said, Oh Boy, you must get lots of slaps. Arthur replied yes I do, but I also get lots of passionate sex.

The Meat Pies

Another story my father told me was about the meat pies.

In Kelty we had a co-operative grocery store, located quite close to where we lived. When you became a member of the Co-operative, you were given a book, on which you could charge merchandise up to a certain value, and which you would pay for, once a month. Mrs Brown was a member of the Cooperative, and used her book to charge merchandise, for which she would pay for, every two months. Well, one day Mrs. Brown needed a few groceries so she asked my dad, who was only a young boy at the time, if he would run an errand. My dad said he would, so Mrs. Brown gave him a list of groceries to get. My dad said, what about the money for them Mrs. Brown? And she replied, just tell the store to charge them to my account, and I'll get the book marked up to date, the next time I am in the store. My dad and several of his pals set off to get the groceries When they arrived at the store, they had to wait their turn to be served. When they were being served, they got all the items on Mrs Brown's list. However, by this time they felt a little hungry, so they decided that they would all have a meat pie each, which was duly put on Mrs Brown's bill. Mrs Brown got into the habit of sending the boys for her groceries at least once a week, sometimes twice. She never noticed the extra items on her bill, when she went to pay her account. Sometimes the boys would get bottles of lemonade with the meat pies. This went on for a long time, and Mrs Brown never did find out about the meat pies.

My Most Embarrassing Moment

Many years ago, I worked for the Hudson's bay company in their Winnipeg store; I will never forget the experience of being in my first fashion show.

The Bay was going to hold a fashion show for their staff in the large auditorium, after store hours. Six men were required for the show. The idea was to dress the men in costumes, showing where the designer got the idea for the dresses. Being of dark complexion, they of course asked me to wear a matador's costume, to which I agreed. Well, the night came and I, together with the other men, were behind the stage, all dressed up in our different costumes. Finally the moment of truth arrived and I had to climb up a few steps, pass through a curtain and on to the stage. The moment I walked on to the stage, I was hit by blinding lights and realized that the auditorium was packed with woman, staff members. There were hundreds of them. The place was in an uproar. I looked so funny that everyone in the place started to howl with laughter. There I was, walking across the stage in this matador costume, with my skinny legs bare to the world. The laughter grew into a crescendo and lasted what I imagined at the time, to be at least ten minutes There I was looking up at the ceiling, trying to remain cool and calm, while whistling under my breath. Finally the laughter stopped and I was left standing at one side of the stage, while models in their dresses paraded on and off the stage. All of a sudden the next man came out on the stage and the laughter started all over again. One by one each of the men came out and the laughter would start all over again. Eventually the show was over and the six men slunk off the stage, thoroughly embarrassed and humiliated. Even today, forty years later. When anyone mentions a fashion show, I turn pale and get ready to run.

The Trip To Edinburgh

Edinburgh train station is very large, and it is completely covered with glass, there is a road that leads right down the hill into the station and taxis' and cars can drive down this road right into the station to drop off or pick up passengers. Being so large it has of course, quite a few shops all selling different merchandise.

One day at work, Jimmy told his mates that on Saturday, he was going to visit Edinburgh for the first time.

Saturday came and Jimmy took the train to Edinburgh, his pal's wished him luck, and off Jimmy went.

Monday morning came and Jimmy was back at work in the pit. Naturally, his pals wanted to know how he had got on in Edinburgh. Jimmy said Oh I thoroughly enjoyed myself, Edinburgh is a great place to visit, and did you know it's all covered with glass. Jimmy didn't know it, but he had never been out of the railway station.

The Mark

Jimmy Humble was a young man who lived in Kelty, and worked down the local coal mine.

One day as Jimmy was about to go down the pit, his pal said to him, Jimmy don't forget we're going on the town tonight, so I'll wait for you after work. The only problem is how will I know if you are up the pit, or still working. To which Jimmy replied, that's easy to know, because if I'm up the pit first, I'll put a chalk mark on this wall, and if your up first, you rub it off.

The Encounter

My next story about Jimmy, concerned the time before he got married. He is credited with this story, whether it is true or not.

It seem that several of his mates were going to a dance in Edinburgh, the following Saturday, and they asked Jimmy if he wanted to come along. At the dance Jimmy met a girl who lived in Edinburgh. They got on very well, so Jimmy asked to see her home. They left the dance a bit early and Jimmy took her home. When they arrived there, the girl asked Jimmy if he would like to come in for a little while. The girl made Jimmy a meal, and they had a few drinks together. After a period of time, Jimmy looked at his watch and said to the girl, I have been enjoying myself so much, that I completely forgot the time, and now I have missed the last train back to the Kelty. The girl thought for a moment then said that's no problem, you can stay here tonight, and catch a train to Kelty tomorrow. They of course slept in the same bed that night and the next morning Jimmy caught a train to Kelty. On Monday morning Jimmy was back at work in the pit, and his mates were anxious to hear the details of his encounter. Jimmy told them, how he had been given a meal and some drinks, and then slept with the girl. Then he said, I've decided to go back to Edinburgh next Saturday. His mates then asked him why he was going back to Edinburgh again. Jimmy replied, that girl, I think she's a sure thing.

The Drink of Water

Jimmy Humble got married, and about a year later, his wife was expecting a baby.

One day the mid-wife called on Jimmy's wife, who was in bed, because she was due to have the baby anytime. Jimmies wife said to the mid-wife, thank god you're here, I am dying of thirst, and Jimmy will not give me a drink of water. The mid-wife gave her a drink, then went downstairs and said to Jimmy, why would you not give your wife a drink of water, to which Jimmy replied, do you think I want to drown my baby.

Winter

The weeping snow was silent
Trees had turned to white
The raging wind was violent
As day turned into night

The angry sky tinged with red
Clouds were wild and bold
The autumn leaves were lying dead
Winter's taken hold

There Was A Young Man From The Dock's

There was a young man from the dock's
Who dressed up in young ladies frocks
He was chaste and demure
Of that much I'm sure
Until he dated some jocks

The Debt

A priest a minister and a rabbi, each borrowed 20,000 dollars from a rich landlord. They all promised faithfully that they would pay back the loan. A few months later however the landlord died and was lying in his coffin prior to the lid being screwed down.

The priest came to the funeral home, went over the coffin and said, thank you for the loan, and placed $20,000 inside the coffin, beside the landlord. A few minutes later the minister came in, went over to the coffin and said, thank you for the loan then placed $20,000 inside the coffin. The rabbi came in a few minutes later, went over to the coffin. He lifted out the $40,000, then put his hand in his pocket, took out his chequebook wrote a cheque for $60,000. He then placed the cheque inside the coffin, next to the landlord and said, thank you for the loan.

How To Commit Murder

John decided to go and see his friend Arthur one day.

They hadn't seen each other for quite a few years. He went to Arthur's house, where Arthur's wife let him in.

Arthur and John talked for a while, then Arthur said, I'm not happy, my wife is driving me crazy. I wish there was some way I could get rid of her. Without being caught. John said, well if you want to get rid of your wife, there is a way to do it, and its quite safe. Arthur said what way is that. John said, if you make love to your wife, morning, noon, and night, for three months. I guarantee you, she will die. Arthur thanked John and then John left.

Ten weeks later, john decided to visit Arthur again. When he knocked on the door, the wife let him in, she told John that Arthur was in the living room. When John went into the living room, he found Arthur wrapped up in shawl, sitting shivering in front of the fire. Arthur was as pale as a ghost. He had lost a lot of weight and his hair had turned white. John could hear Arthur's wife through in the kitchen singing her heart out. John said, your wife seems to be very happy. And Arthur replied, yes, but little does she know that she has only two weeks to live.

A Way of Life

In the beginning there was nothing
In the end there is nothing.
It's what we do with our lives in between that counts.
My advice is to live for pleasure.
Take pleasure out of the many small things we do each day.
Take pleasure out of a beautiful sunny day;
Treat it as though it were your last.
Take pleasure out of beautiful scenery and the wonder of it all.
Take pleasure out of going for a walk and observing all of God's
creatures on the way.
If you have to work, treat it as an experience and that goes for the
many bad things that happen to us in our lives.
If you cannot get pleasure from it, then treat it as an experience.
If you look for pleasure in things, you will find it,
you will be happier than you have ever been.
Much more than you can imagine.
Just try it. What do you have to lose.

The Distribution

A priest, a minister and a rabbi, were talking one day, on how they distribute the money that comes in to their churches from the congregation.

The priest said well, what I do is throw all the money into the air, and the money that comes down that is showing a head, I send to the Vatican, the tails I keep.

The minister said I do almost the same thing. I throw the money into the air and what comes down heads up, I keep.

The rabbi said well I do something similar too. I throw all the money into the air, and I tell God to keep what he wants and I keep the money that falls to the ground.

The Traveler

John who lived in Edinburgh was going down, to London by car. Arthur, his friend said, there is a little town this side of Leeds and in this town is a restaurant who have a policy for first time customers, that if they cannot serve you with what you order, they will give you twenty pounds. John then started off for London. He was traveling by car and he was in the Yorkshire Moors When the car broke down. He cursed the car for breaking down and started to walk. He got about a 100 yards when he saw the dim outline of a house away in the distance. He made for the house and got about half way there when, all the lights went out. He cursed the person who put out the lights, however he could still see the dark outline of the house. He finally made it to the door, and he knocked on it. The door opened and a little boy stood there. Is your father in, John said. No said the boy, he came out when my mother came in. Is your mother in then, John said. No she came out when my sister came in. Is your sister in then said john. No she came out when I came in, said the boy. Truly frustrated by this time, John said what kind of a house is this. The boy replied, oh this is the Outhouse. John finally got the help he wanted. Got the car started and finally made his way to the small town that Arthur had told him about. Once he was in the town he soon found the restaurant, went in and sat down. A waitress came over to take his order. What will you have she said. John remembered what Arthur had told him about the twenty pounds, so he said I'll have some spiders liver on toast. The waitress went away and about five minutes later the manager came over to him. The manager said did you order spider's liver on toast. John said that he had. The manager then said to him. We have a custom here, that with first time customers, if they order anything that we don't have, we give them twenty pounds. Here's your twenty pounds, we've run out of toast.

The Aviator

A British airman was shot down over Germany during the war. He was in hospital for about two weeks, when the German doctor came to him and said. I'm very sorry but I'm afraid we are going to have to cut off your left leg. The airman was disappointed at first, then said to the doctor, can I ask you to do me a favour. When the German planes are bombing England, could you have them throw the leg out over London.   The doctor replied I don't know, I'll have to ask the commandant. The next day the doctor came back to him and said the commandant say yes, we will do it.   A couple of weeks later the doctor came to him again and said. I'm very sorry but we will have to take off your right arm.   The airman then said will you do me another favour, can you have my arm thrown out a plane over London just as they did with my leg. The doctor replied I don't know, I'll have to ask the commandant.   Next day the doctor came back to him and said. The commandant say's yes. A few weeks went by and the doctor came back to him again and said. I'm very sorry but we'll have to take off you left arm. The airman said can we make the same arrangement as before and drop it over London. The doctor replied I don't know I'll have to ask the commandant. Next day he came back and said, the commandant say's yes. A month went by and the doctor came back to the airman and said, I'm very sorry but we're going to have to cut off your right leg. Naturally the airman was very disappointed but said to the doctor, can we make the same arrangement as before to which the doctor replied I don't know I'll have to ask the commandant. Next day the doctor came back and said I'm sorry, the commandant say's no. But why not asked the airman. The doctor replied, he thinks your trying to escape.

Depression

When I feel depressed and sad
The world seems dark and gloomy
I remember the good times I've had
When luck was coming to me.

Depression is a state of mind
It makes the world seem mad
I forget about the other kind
The good times that I've had

So when I'm feeling very bad
And problems they are pressing
I remember of the child I had
And thank God for his blessing

The Cemetery

Visiting a cemetery
I saw tombstones in a row
Reminding me of love ones past
The ones I used to know

I knew that I must be brave
And from the spot I hurried
Because I saw an empty grave
The place where I'll be buried.

Brigham Young

You know about Brigham Young who was a Mormon leader.

He always used to say I don't care how you bring them,
just bring em young.

The Making Of Scotland

In the beginning when the world was being created

God was in his chambers
Working on some plans
When in came angel Gabriel
With spare time on his hands

What are you doing Lord
Gabe said it with affection
I'm creating a new country said God
Without an imperfection

You are full of anticipation
But you'll see when my plan is unfurled
I'm creating Scotland a brand new nation
The best country in the world

It will be a beautiful land
One you will adore
Its beaches will have lots of sand
And many miles of shore
Majestic mountains that reach the sky
Forests with greenery
A haven where all birds can fly
Amid this scenery

It will have spacious glens
Filled with purple heather
A place where men can be men
And clans can get together

It will have coal in the ground
And oil beneath the sea
A haggis that is plump and round
A nectar they call tea

Its golf courses will be lush and green
And rivers filled with fish
A promised land fit for a Queen
As good as you can wish

There's nothing bad I must confess
But just you wait and see
I'll put a monster in loch ness
And bagpipes that seem off key

Hold on God I know your kind
And your giving Scotland lots
But your giving the best of all mankind
Don't you think your too generous to these Scots

No I'm not doing them any favours
Though Scotland is a gem
Wait 'till you see the terrible neighbours
That I'm giving them

A cup of tea

I was talking to my brother jack the other day and he reminded me of the time i tried to help my mother with her housework. I was only 10 years old at the time and in our living room in Adams Terrace, we had a large beautiful fireplace. The fireplace itself was not too big, because it was part of what we called "the ranger" the range was approximately 5 feet wide and made of iron and steel. Most of the range was made of a black iron and the edges were made of steel, silver in appearance. On one side of the range it had an oven, complete with a black metal door. The front was also black. Every so often my mother would use a black lead polish mixed with black tea to clean and polish the range. Well, one day I decided to clean and polish the range. My mother had gone out shopping so I thought I would give her a nice surprise when she got home. I got out the polish, mixed it with black tea and started to work. I proceeded to put the mixture on the range, every inch of it. However when I started to shine it up there was something wrong. I couldn't get it to shine at all and it was very sticky. I tried everything, but whenever I touched it, it only made the situation worse. It was a horrible mess. I was in the middle of this fiasco when my mother came home. She took one look at the range and asked me what had happened to it. When I told her what I had tried to do, she wasn't angry with me and thanked me for trying to help. She then took a basin with hot water and started to wash the range. Once the sticky mess had been washed off and dried she then applied a fresh mixture of black lead and tea and polished up the range until it was beautiful again. A few days later I discovered what I had done wrong. I had mixed the black lead and the black tea alright but I had made one mistake, I had added sugar to the tea!!

Canada

Canada a large nation
as large as you will find
has created the situation
to welcome all mankind

Immigrants there are some
who know in this great land
on the day that they come
will get a helping hand

On arrival to our shore
many are glad to be alive
when they walk through our door
will get the chance to thrive

They know this is a land of peace
there is no need to hurry
here all their dangers cease
and do not have to worry

So Canada we salute you
for all that you have done
people get a life that's new
and a chance to have some fun.

First footing

This is a story
One that you should know
About a Scottish custom
Many years ago

The people way back then
Where mostly of good cheer
They celebrated Christmas
And first footed at new year

Christmas was for children
That much we did perceive
And so went willingly to bed
On every Christmas eve

But we all knew that New Year
Was grownups time to play
They celebrated auld lang syne
And New Year's hogmanay

First footing was a custom
The time to visit friends
To take a bottle of liquor
And taste each others blends

They waited until midnight
On every old years night
Then went out first footing
Until the dawn's early light

If you were dark, it was good luck
If not, you carried coal
This strange Scottish custom
Was ingrained upon your soul

And so it came to pass one year
The hour it was quiet late
I decided to go first footing
Although I was just eight

So armed with my blackcurrant wine
Clutched firmly in my hand
I stepped into the darkness
And into no mans land

My immediate goal on that dark night
Was a Mr. and Mrs. Bain
Who lived in a council house
Just down the darkened lane

The wind it howled, the dogs they growled
As I went on my way
I stuck it out, without a shout
My feet, they felt like clay

And then at last, I was aghast
I didn't know the time
I waited outside their door
For signs of auld lang syne

Then all at once, in the night
I heard a Trombone play
And when I heard that lovely tune
I knew it was New Years day

I stepped up to the door and knocked
The door it opened wide
Smiling faces said come in
And so I stepped inside

The first thing that I noticed
The fire was burning bright
A table filled with goodies
It was a welcome sight

Madiera cake, red port wine
Shortbread by the score
I thought I was in heaven
Who could ask for anything more

I took a seat and at my feet
I feline settled down
The house was full of laughter
The best place in the town

I think I stayed an hour or more
Of that I'm not quite sure
By this time I was getting tired
First footing lost it's lure

I bade all my friends goodbye
Then set of in the night
I had a lovely feeling
The world was quite alright

When I got home, I said goodnight
Then shook my sleepy head
I gave my Mom and Dad a kiss
And toddled of to bed

Oor Granny
(Forever in our hearts)

Full of love, Laughter and care would describe oor Gran.
She loved her bingo, shopping and cleaning but most of
all she loved THE GANG as Di would say,
Lisa, Laura, Lindy, Grant, Amie, Calum, Eve
and not forgetting the pup Harvey Boy.
She was like oor 2nd Mum, we all loved her
buttered toast and hame made chips. We will treasure all
the happy memories forever such as the holidays we
went on, the shopping trips, oor cups of tea and a blether,
watching "Dora the Explora" with Eve and many many
more. We could go on forever, as all the memories are
happy ones, which will never be forgotten.
We look up to the sky now and know the brightest
star is you Gran as you shone out from the rest, as you
were the very best.

Sweet dreams, God bless

Love U always

THE GANG
xxxxxxxx

TRIBUTE TO ARTIST
"MY NATIVE LAND"

THOMAS "FRANK" McCORMICK
29/12/1946 - 16/1/2011

Frank was born in Ayr and lived Duncan of Jordonstone College Ayr Academy. Frank played in due to the work commitment give up playing the pipes, but there till he attended the of Art in Dundee when he left a pipe band but unfortunately at the college he was forced to he always loved music.

He studied at the college for 3 fine art. He trained as a field for a year. However he him and he then joined the years and gained a diploma in teacher and worked in that decided teaching was not for police force.

After his police training at Tulliallan Police Training College he served his time in the police in various areas in West Fife, including Burntisland, Dalgety Bay, Inverkeithing and Dunfermline. He served in the police for 30 years and was thought of as a tough but fair minded "bobby"who stood no nonsense but was willing to listen and help people. He gained a couple of nicknames during his life, "glovsie" as he badly injured his right thumb, whilst in the police, and had to wear a glove like support on it. His other nickname was "tasker" which arose from the initials of his name Thomas Slater Kerr.

After Frank retired from the police force he still felt that he had something to give to the community and became a Community Behaviour Management Officer at Inverkeithing High School. He held this post for 4 years and his common sense approach, communication skills, fair mindedness and no nonsense attitude earned the respect of teachers and pupils alike.

Frank never lost his love of art and had kept up with his drawing throughout his working life. When his marriage broke up he joined the Dunfermline Art Club in 2006. He hoped to make art his work but unfortunately his time was cut short by cancer. He was only in the Art Club a few years but he left his mark with his enthusiasm, hard work and commitment to the club. He held a drawing class for 4 years which proved very popular and he held the post of exhibition secretary for 2 years. At exhibitions his drawings proved very popular and he always sold some of his art work and also had work commissioned. He is remembered with great regard for his amazing talent for drawing and for his willingness to offer advice and help to anyone in the club who sought his help.

He bore his illness in the last year of his life with great courage and fortitude and did not want a fuss and so told as few people as possible how ill he was and got on with his life as best he could. He is survived by his daughter Lisa and son Kevin. He will be greatly missed by his family and friends and will be remembered as a very talented artist and a good and honourable man.

Jock the Editor was very sad and upset that Frank did not live to see "My Native Land" published. In the last few weeks of his life Frank was always asking if the book was out yet. Jock had enquired about details of funeral arrangements and was informed there would be no funeral. Frank had donated his body to Medical Science and Research.

SUMMARY OF EDITORS CAREER

Kelty Primary 1946-1952
Beath High School 1952-1956
Apprentice Electrical Fitter 1956-1961
Electrical Fitter 1961-1963 on Destroyers all at Rosyth Dockyard
Finance Department 1963-88 until voluntary retirement Jan 1988 due to ill health.

I married my girlfriend Janie Tod in 1961. Janie was eighteen and I was twenty. I had courted Janie from the day she turned fifteen and we were blessed with three daughters and a son. We had been married forty six years when Janie died suddenly in October 2006. We had been due to fly to Spain on the morning of her death. In the 1960's because the four of my family had come along quite quickly, to supplement my wages I had many part time jobs, Casino Croupier, Cocktail Barman, Waiter, and Chef. From 1990-1997 General Hand in Naval Stores at Rosyth Dockyard until made redundant in 1997, then labouring on Nuclear Submarines 1998-1999 when I had a stroke in April 1999 and suffered from depression from 1999-2005. I only came out of the depression about eighteen months before my wife's death and since then I took up fishing, raised money for various charities and regularly work a twenty hour day.

JOCK WHITELAW